PLANETS IN OUR SOLAR SYSTEM

Learn About JUPITER!

BY NATALIE HUMPHREY

Enslow PUBLISHING

DISCOVER!

Please visit our website, www.enslow.com. For a free color catalog of all our high-quality books, call toll free 1-800-398-2504 or fax 1-877-980-4454.

Cataloging-in-Publication Data

Names: Humphrey, Natalie.
Title: Learn about Jupiter! / Natalie Humphrey.
Description: New York : Enslow Publishing, 2024. | Series: Planets in our solar system | Includes index.
Identifiers: ISBN 9781978533523 (pbk.) | ISBN 9781978533530 (library bound) | ISBN 9781978533547 (ebook)
Subjects: LCSH: Jupiter (Planet)–Juvenile literature.
Classification: LCC QB661.H857 2024 | DDC 523.45–dc23

Portions of this work were originally authored by Daisy Allyn and published as *Jupiter: The Largest Planet.* All new material in this edition authored by Natalie Humphrey.

Published in 2024 by
Enslow Publishing
2544 Clinton Street
Buffalo, NY 14224

Designer: Andrea Davison-Bartolotta
Editor: Natalie Humphrey

Photo credits: Cover (Jupiter), p. 1 (Jupiter) joshimerbin/Shutterstock.com; cover (top), p. 1 (top), series art (backgrounds) Jurik Peter/ Shutterstock.com; series art (lens flare) andruxevich/Shutterstock.com; p.4 Natee Jitthammachai/Shutterstock.com; pp. 5, 11 Vadim Sadovski/Shutterstock.com; p. 7 shooarts/Shutterstock.com; p. 9 NASA/JPL-Caltech/SwRI/MSSS/Kevin M. Gill; p. 13 NASA/JPL/ SwRI/MSSS; image processing by Gerald Eichstädt; p. 15 Pavel Gabzdyl/Shutterstock.com; p. 17 ManuMata/Shutterstock.com; p. 19 Elena11/Shutterstock.com; p. 21 Beyond Space/Shutterstock.com.

Printed in the United States of America

CPSIA compliance information: Batch #CS24ENS: For further information contact Enslow Publishing, at 1-800-398-2504.

CONTENTS

Boldface words appear in Words to Know.

All About JUPITER!

Jupiter is the largest planet in our **solar system**. It's so big, you could fit nearly 1,300 Earths inside of it! But that's not the only thing that's great about the fifth planet from the sun. Jupiter is so large, you can even see it without a **telescope**.

Jupiter is 480 million miles (780 million km) from the sun.

A Year on JUPITER

Jupiter takes a long time to **orbit** the sun. Just one orbit for Jupiter takes almost 12 Earth years! Even though Jupiter's year is long, one day for Jupiter is very short. It takes about 10 hours for Jupiter to spin completely!

Jupiter is close to 11 times wider than planet Earth!

The Great RED SPOT

Jupiter looks like it's covered in stripes from far away, but those stripes are really clouds! Jupiter has strong winds and many storms that cover its skies. The largest storm on Jupiter is called the Great Red Spot. It's usually the largest storm in the solar system.

The Great Red Spot has been a storm for at least 340 years.

A Gas GIANT

Jupiter is also called a gas giant. Instead of having a thick, rocky crust like the Earth, Jupiter's surface is made out of gases! Beneath these gases could be Jupiter's **core**. Scientists believe Jupiter's core is possibly made out of ice, rock, and metal.

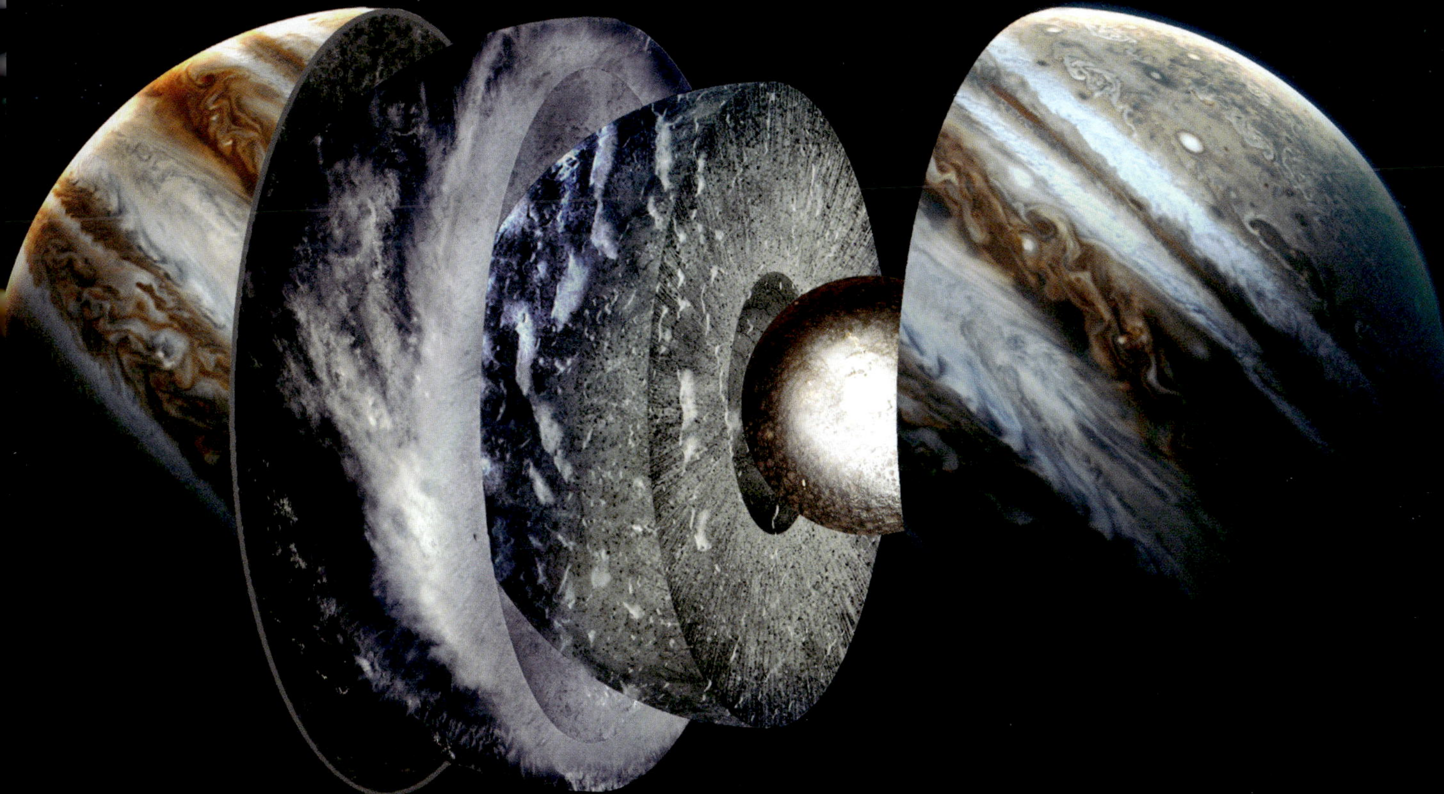

Jupiter's core could be much larger than the entire planet Earth!

Failed STAR

Jupiter is made of mostly **hydrogen** and **helium** gas. Our sun, a star, is also made out of hydrogen and helium. This has made scientists believe that Jupiter might have been a star that never **ignited**.

Scientists believe Jupiter was too small to become a star!

Many MOONS

Jupiter has a lot more moons than Earth! Jupiter is so large, there are about 80 moons orbiting it. Jupiter's moon Ganymede (GA-nih-meed) is the biggest moon in our solar system. Ganymede is so big, it's larger than the planet Mercury!

It takes Ganymede 172 hours to orbit Jupiter.

The Rings of JUPITER

Saturn isn't the only planet that has rings! Even though Jupiter's rings are hard to see, a space **probe** showed Jupiter had them in 1979. Unlike Saturn's rings, Jupiter's rings are made of mostly dust and small pieces of rock.

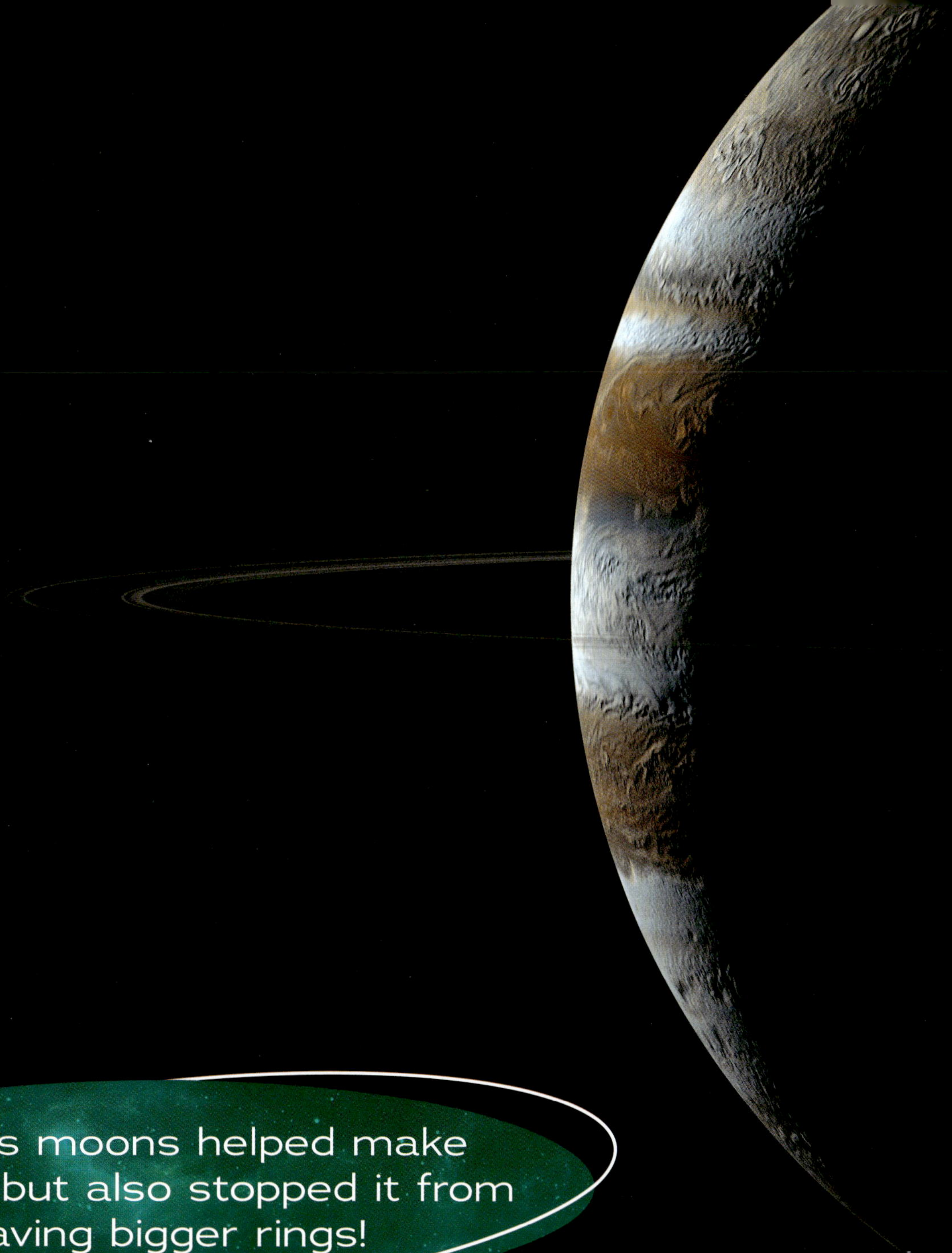

Jupiter's moons helped make its rings, but also stopped it from having bigger rings!

Strong GRAVITY

Jupiter has such a strong **gravitational pull**, it sucks in many small objects from space. In fact, Jupiter has around 200 times the number of space object collisions, or crashes, as Earth! Some of these objects, like asteroids, get stuck in Jupiter's gravitational pull and become new moons.

Because it pulls in so much stuff, some scientists call Jupiter the solar system's vacuum cleaner!

Into Deep SPACE

Even though no human has walked on Jupiter, we've still seen pictures of it up close! **Spacecraft** including the Voyager 1 and 2 probes have passed by Jupiter and sent photos back to Earth. Because of these spacecraft, we're still discovering more about this gas giant!

VOYAGER SPACE PROBE

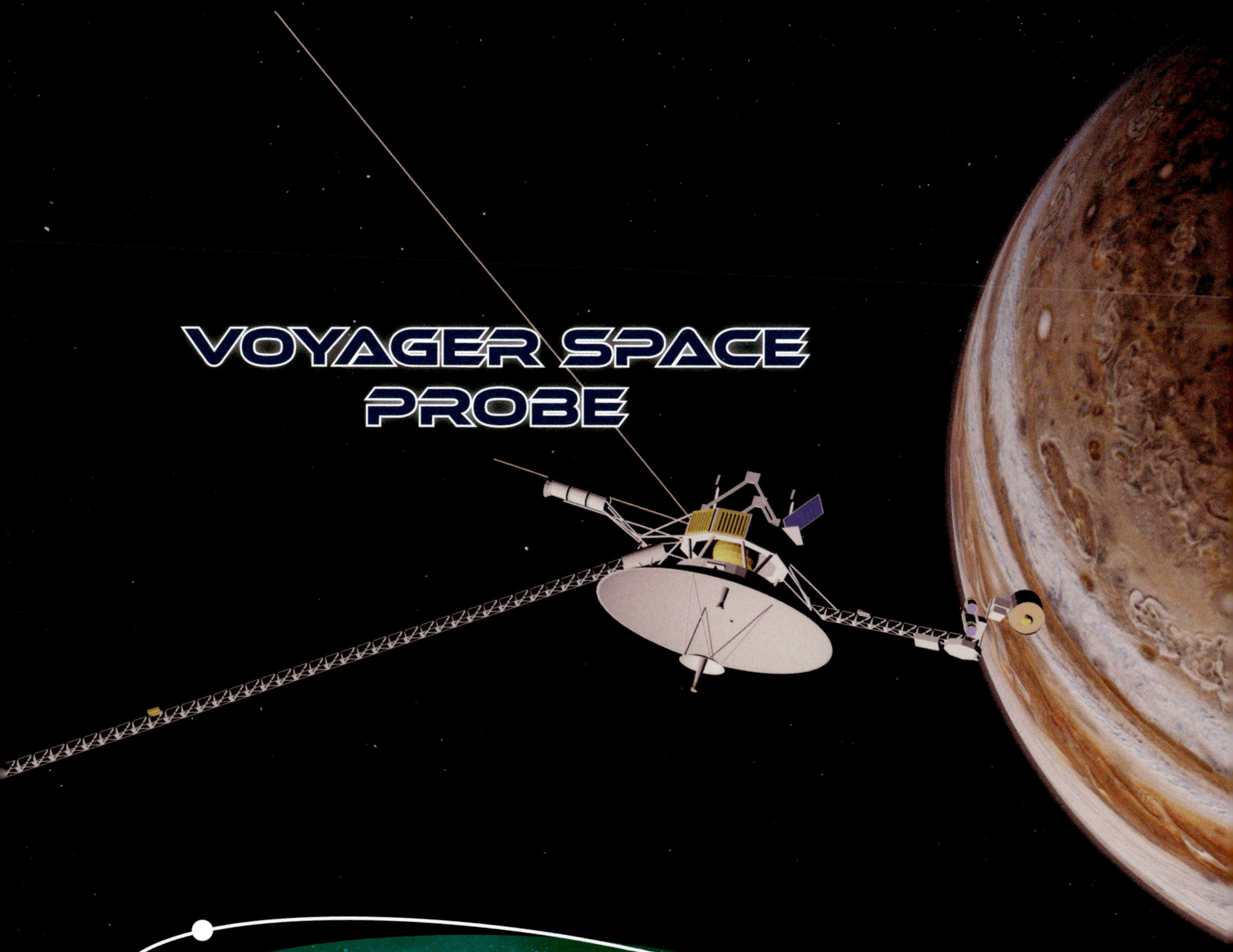

The Voyager space probes were launched in 1977 and are still working today!

WORDS TO KNOW

core: The central part of something.

gravitational pull: The force that causes objects with large masses to be attracted to each other.

helium: One of the most common gases in our solar system.

hydrogen: A common gas. Also, the most common matter in the solar system.

ignite: To cause something to suddenly burn.

orbit: To travel in a circle or oval around something.

probe: An unmanned spaceship.

solar system: The sun and all the space objects that orbit it, including the planets and their moons.

spacecraft: A human-made object that travels through space.

telescope: A tool that makes faraway objects look bigger and closer.